Withdrawn/ABCL

D0556554

THE
NARROW CIRCLE

NATHAN HOKS

PENGUIN BOOKS

PENGUIN BOOKS
Published by the Penguin Group
Penguin Group (USA) Inc., 375 Hudson Street,
New York, New York 10014, USA

USA | Canada | UK | Ireland | Australia | New Zealand | India | South Africa | China
Penguin Books Ltd, Registered Offices: 80 Strand, London WC2R 0RL, England
For more information about the Penguin Group visit penguin.com

First published in Penguin Books 2013

Copyright © Nathan Hoks, 2013
All rights reserved. No part of this product may be reproduced, scanned, or distributed in any printed or electronic
form without permission. Please do not participate in or encourage piracy of copyrighted materials
in violation of the author's rights. Purchase only authorized editions.

Page 7 constitutes an extension of this copyright page.

Image credits appear on page 83.

LIBRARY OF CONGRESS CATALOGING-IN-PUBLICATION DATA
Hoks, Nathan.
[Poems. Selections]
The narrow circle / Nathan Hoks.
pages ; cm.—(National poetry series)
ISBN 978-0-14-312373-6
I. Title.
PS3608.O48285N37 2013
811'.6—dc23
2013006561

Printed in the United States of America

1 3 5 7 9 10 8 6 4 2

Set in GranjonLT Std
Designed by Sabrina Bowers

For Teddy

ACKNOWLEDGMENTS

Thank you to the editors of the following venues in which some of these poems first appeared, often in different versions: *Boston Review*; *Colorado Review*; *Crazyhorse*; *Forklift, Ohio*; *H_ngm_n*; *jubilat*; *The New Megaphone*; *Poem, Home: An Anthology of Ars Poetica*; *SCUD*.

"Infinite Interior" appeared on a broadside for the Pop Mirror-Shaped Reading in Madison, Wisconsin. Thank you to Lewis Freedman and Andy Gricevich.

Thank you to my family for their tolerance and encouragement, and thank you to everyone whose spirit and intelligence helped along these poems, especially Nikki Flores, James Shea, Chad Chmielowicz, Chris Hund, Joel Craig, Joseph Bienvenu, Jorge Sánchez, Vieve Kaplan, Leora Fridman, Catherine Theis, Jill Magi, Maureen Ewing, Larry Sawyer, Michael Anichini, Eugene Sampson, Sarah Green, Jared Stanley, and Kate Hollander. Thank you also to Paul Slovak at Penguin and Stephanie Stio at the National Poetry Series.

CONTENTS

THE INTERIOR

Flight to the Interior   *3*

Shadow of the Interior   *4*

Birth of the Interior   *5*

Operation White Out   *6*

Personality Test   *7*

Invisible Barrier Syndrome   *10*

Chair of the Interior   *11*

Robot of the Interior   *12*

The Reality of the Interior   *13*

Charles Dickens of the Interior   *14*

Mouth of the Interior   *15*

Birds of the Interior   *18*

People of the Interior   *19*

Spiral of the Interior   *20*

Infinite Interior   *27*

Lily of the Interior   *30*

Family of the Interior   *31*

Film of the Interior   *32*

Institution of the Interior   *33*

God of the Interior   *35*

Farewell, Interior   *37*

Hôtel l'Intérieur   *39*

THE EXTERIOR

Sandwich of the Exterior   *45*

Family of the Exterior   *47*

Winter of the Exterior   *48*

Message of the Exterior   *49*

Building the Sandbox of the Exterior   *50*

Outline of the Exterior (The Sun)   *51*

Candelabra   *54*

The Architect and the Hat   *56*

Spores of the Exterior   *60*

Marigold of the Exterior   *61*

Barometer of the Exterior   *64*

Twitch of the Exterior   *65*

Sky of the Exterior   *66*

Mouth of the Exterior   *70*

Anatomy of the Exterior   *71*

Steam of the Exterior   *72*

Edge of the Exterior   *73*

Animal of the Exterior   *74*

Apple Tree of the Exterior   *75*

Heart of the Exterior   *78*

Letter of the Exterior   *79*

Mind of the Exterior   *81*

Image Credits   *83*

They told me that I had five senses to inclose me up.
And they inclos'd my infinite brain into a narrow circle,
And sunk my heart into the Abyss, a red round globe hot burning
Till all from life I was obliterated and erased.

—WILLIAM BLAKE

THE
INTERIOR

FLIGHT TO THE INTERIOR

I've got secrets I'm about to leave in the river
And it makes me feel homeless to stand here
Having to think them through.
Silence yourself, says the tree line—
You are miniature, absorbing
Time on your way to the end of the tunnel.
You are about to enter an orange plain
And the sound in your head will be
A car starting in the rain. You will fill yourself
With pockets. You will file your nails
Until the heart of your ghost fills with glowing juice.
Finally you feel fully washed of your self,
Blown into several pieces of sky, transparent
But also a bloblike raindrop.
For the rest of the day you will glue
Blue and green squares to the tree trunks.
Every rotting leaf is a form of speculation
You have inherited from the raindrop.
When the shadow splatters, the thing itself splatters.
All of us become the river.

SHADOW OF THE INTERIOR

My friend Michael always carries
His chair from house to house.
He calls this chair his heart, his warm
Beeping heart that he cannot shake
From his hands no matter how hard
He shakes them. Imagine, he says,
Imagine having to look at your inner life
Always in your hands, always pointing
The direction from place to place
Until you cannot stand it. One day
You are in a desert where there is
Simply no context for your feelings.
A rhythm rattles your head.
Light sneaks quickly into your eyes
And you cannot tell yourself from sky.
You need a place to lie down, a place
To bore into. You will be happy to
Have your chair. You will clutch its
Thin legs and think about the moon.
A little bit of rock and mud under your
Feet reminds you there was a lake here once.
Lucky you. You see everything inside out.

BIRTH OF THE INTERIOR

The oysters I did not eat are in the fridge
Dreaming of the ocean they did not mean
To leave. They came here on an
Airplane, in many ways like my wife
Who is washing her face in the bathroom
That makes your face feel like it is
Shrinking so you try to get out. If you stand
Up too fast you feel blood running
Circles in your head, tightening the skin around
Your nose and cheekbones. Perhaps your hair
Grows a little. In the mirror you don't
Notice major changes but you feel
Something large poking its soft head
Through your chest. You are excited
For the new installment. You run to
Tell your friends to get out their cameras.
They have never heard of cameras. You
Walk across the couch to the window
Where the raindrops have settled
Into a little pool on the sill. You are
Half of everything you see. The indiscretion
Pulverizes your insides. You have to wear
A shiny fur hat to cover up the pieces.

OPERATION WHITE OUT

My friend John is always carrying on
About the laundry detergent. His neighbors
Have built tall fences. When he walks
Into a party the host turns up the music.
I try to cheer him up, invite him over
For jelly donuts. His sullen face bothers
My dogs. His bloodshot eyes seem to drip
On their egg-white fur. I try to distract him
By sharing my theory that over the years
The sky's shade of blue has been
Gradually lightening so that soon
The sky will be white all the time.
You won't want to bleach your undershirts.
You won't care about the enzymes,
How they work away at the marinara
On your cloth napkin. And the lake
Of soluble phosphates will fill with
Algal blooms and kill the fish and plants.
The same green spot is growing inside me.

PERSONALITY TEST

Everyone tells me I look like Jim.
Jim, I say, who the hell is Jim? In truth
I know him, but I'm feeling anxious
About these accusations. I have to flip
Through a stack of magazines just to
Work up the courage to go to bed. And
When I awake I'm not certain I'm in
The right room. My fear is assuaged
When I see Jim's portrait hanging
Over the dresser. I reach for the feathers
I keep on the nightstand. Their silky
Texture teases my insides, begs them
To come out. Another tissue wriggles
And glides its cursive across the wall.
If I were to close the curtain more dust
Would appear around the rim
Of my water glass. I can't drink any more.
My insides will be washed away.

Finally you feel fully washed of your self

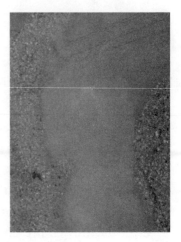

Lucky you, you see everything inside out

Tell your friends to get out their cameras

My insides will be washed away

INVISIBLE BARRIER SYNDROME

All the good baby names have been taken
Says my wife who refuses to have a child
But can't stop playing with the stuffed zebra
That lives in the box beside our couch.
The shadows brush by her face as if refusing
To let her pass. But a baby does not need
A name and I can imagine it on a large wheel
Rolling through the door. A man in overalls
Will probably be behind it with his cell
Phone going off and a pigeon feather in
His ear, which will make us cringe, but we'll
Be cool, we'll play along. We'll pull out the couch
And add a picture of a truck to the wall.
No one but babies believes in walls
But there they are and we cannot avoid
Walking around them. Walls in my house,
Walls on the street. When there are enough
Walls my wife and I stand in the middle and call it
The inside. A leaf is growing out of our face.

CHAIR OF THE INTERIOR

The chair is my *hombre*, my shadow, my humming stone and
curvature. It says *yes* and I dress it in tissues, supple to its nicks
and gashes. I meant to save it from fissures, from virtue, from
nature. My *hombre, mi amor*, I can't remember life without
you. Did I have one? One perhaps, under a brackish master,
all queasy and nebulous, supine and lost in transmutation so
as to permeate the bread, *even* the bread subsumed by lifeless
vapors. The sky is a kind of bread, all-permeable, blue *amigo*, a
package to unpack at a rocky summit. *Hombre* chair, *hermano*
sky, they become one, they hoist me, the air thins, and from
this angle I see a panther hunting mules. And though it pains
me, I stop myself from stopping it.

ROBOT OF THE INTERIOR

My robot is a challenged acquaintance. He wears blue in the morning, dreams of cigars, speaks often of the azure. To him people are pink and pukish and dull and distrustful. When we look at each other we squint and say "soup," or "s'up?" Though we never shake hands and absolutely refuse to call each other by name. I've been asking him to keep a diary or paint a picture. I try to explain the ecosystem but he only hears a squirting sound. "Are you unhappy?" he asks, and although I know he means it, I can only point to the ceiling and smile.

THE REALITY OF THE INTERIOR

is a flower turning toward the sun on a day there is no sun.
I drink a lot of water and try to sit still. My insides jiggle a
little—just enough to make me ill. I look outside: still no sun.
Even after the rain, nothing. When my wife comes home, I
close the shades and go to bed. When I wake up, a speckled
flower is peering through the window.

CHARLES DICKENS OF THE INTERIOR

It was midnight when I heard the voice on the radio. Ice must have been turning into water on the roof for I could also hear a painful groaning coming from above. Inside there was painful groaning too—maybe that's an exaggeration though I feel to a certain extent that painful groaning is a characteristic state of being inside. Perhaps this stems from the winter when we kept the heat too high and I was always waking up in the middle of the night soaked in sweat so we'd have to change the sheets before getting back to sleep. I was reading a novel by Charles Dickens, I don't remember which, and it occurred to me that reading itself is a kind of sleep. The text and the heart rate work in chorus. An image flashes through the head. *Charles Dickens Charles Dickens*. His voice was never on the radio but I hear it now and then and it does not give me shivers which you'd expect of a ghost's voice. London fog. That is his voice. And the purple interior of this bedroom. That is his voice too.

MOUTH OF THE INTERIOR

When I hold a spatula
To the lighted lightbulb, the silhouette
Zooms away. The silhouette burns
A mouth inside the mouth. The mouth

Burns an engine in the silhouette.
With this mouth you might say:
Silhouette yourself. With this mouth
You might make other mouths.

You might spend four days kissing.
You might sing and eat at the same time.
This mouth does not fear
The street sweepers, the meter maids,

The parking attendants who piece
Quilts out of left-behind seatbelts.
With this mouth a bird rises and flares out,
The wind swims by like seaweeds,

An electrical charge and the wind
And a lantern around your neck.
Mouth around your neck.
Neck around your neck.

The silhouette comes back like a cape.
Mouth eats poem. Falls from rafters.
Lightbulb beside the house, house up in flames.

The same green spot is growing inside me

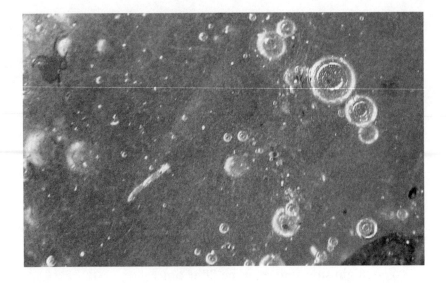

My *hombre, mi amor*

It does not give me the shivers

THE LIBRARY COMPANY OF PHILADELPHIA

A mouth inside the mouth

BIRDS OF THE INTERIOR

On the side street of my heart
In the control room of my silence
In the landfill of my shadow

In the happenstance of the silo
In the spirit of my laundry room
In the water tower of my life

Below the watchtower of my social life
In the fuse box of my empathy
In the fuselage of my ire

Around the archipelago of my apathy
Beneath the corkscrew of my libido
Within the coalition of my slumber

Between the swagger of my oil tanks
On the kite string of the image
Behind the body armor of going on and on

In the cottage of my spectacles
In the cabin of my speechlessness
In the bondage of my voice box

In the cocktail of my inaccuracy
In the cocktail of my appetite
In the cocktail of a steady gaze
In the cocktail of a steady gaze

PEOPLE OF THE INTERIOR

Nathan Hoks is a millipede
With a thousand eyes, sparkling shards
Of glass stabbing at our footwear.
He should be squashed.
He should be flayed.
He should be torn from himself
And made to watch the writhing arms
Strewn across the concrete floor.
He should be born before we talk about him like this.
But Nathan Hoks cannot be killed.
Nathan Hoks will evaporate in the kettle.
Nathan Hoks is a vague hunger.
Nathan Hoks is a 50/50 blend
Gunpowder and guts. Film comes
Whirring out of his mouth.
Rusted screws hold his fingers to his hands.
Flies hang around his buttocks.
Shoots and pods are sprouting from his intestines.
Nathan Hoks is a fork in the egg yolk.
Nathan Hoks is a penitentiary.
Nathan Hoks lives inside himself
Where he is choking on the curtains,
Coughing clouds of dust into the sky.
When he looks in the mirror
He sees brown bile filling a barrel.
His face is a bubble.
His face is a mail bomb.
His handshake is a dragonfly
Fucking itself to death.

SPIRAL OF THE INTERIOR

1

In the first spiral

the blueberries roll out of the bag. We spend an afternoon
picking them up one by one then wiping purple streaks off the
kitchen floor. Outside a robin is looking in.

In all the subsequent spirals

my teeth are pulling at the frontal lobe. A lake forms in the
middle of my face. Another face forms in the bottom of the
lake. Personality sprouts like weeds along the shore. At last
Nathan Hoks is becoming a purple streak.

In some embowered corner

a seedling springs to life. As I approach it enervations take
hold of each limb one at a time. I sink deep into the cushion of
sound where I can hear a bullhorn voice whispering messages
about water. I'll need to eat in a few days. I take a towel and a
toothbrush. Nothing else.

2

In another spiral

I hear the chapel filling with voices. The dust motes scamper
to the windowsills. Another sky slides away revealing that
the gears and wires above us have stalled and are starting
to sparkle. A neighbor puts his hand on my shoulder. The
symptoms begin—I shiver—sleep settles for the foot—etc.

Thin passageways

shaped like white diamonds open in every direction but
Nathan Hoks is not a multitude and cannot splinter to follow
them. I toss an eyelash toward each portal then hang my head
around the bandana, listening.

Zipping the sweater

to the neck I feel myself burrow straight into the ground, my
lips dislodged by mud, my sternum housing a coiled snake,
bodies swallowing bodies, the spiral coming for the face, toes
confused with worms and pebbles.

3

In the only spiral

I awaken to find the bright room drenched in a cleansing agent.
It tastes white, a kind of scintillation that wraps around the
tongue. Children play quietly in the yard. They are wearing red
sweatshirts and bouncing rubber balls. The sky has turned into a
large ball sitting on the porch watching over us.

But after lunch

a symptom returns, namely, I feel that I am holding a poker in
my left hand and I must go from house to house to find a fire
to tend to. I hate ringing the bells

and I ring the bell.

The door creaks open but no one is behind it. The odor of
grass and dandelions comes from the hallway. I stick my head
in and can see that, in the kitchen at the end of the hallway,
someone has left the refrigerator open. I close it and go home.

4

After the yellow feeling

fades from my skin I lie on the grass where I want to shake off
the necklace of droplets. I need to hold on to a spoon or some
object of equal proportion that can simulate the scooping of the
cerebral cortex. I will dig out the illness this way and an ocean
of electrolytes will wash out my intestines.

Three or four

feelings later the spoon wish turns to rain. A ghost finger taps
me on the shoulder but I will not disappear with it into the
oak's bear-shaped shadow. I have to watch this sparrow bounce
and eat in the grass.

The wind pops

the soap bubble, my face disperses with angels of teeth and
loam. The snake sheds its skin, the tree of steam leafs its way
into the sky.

5

The third spiral

gives way to a beeping dump truck which comes and goes
in even waves. I cannot see the construction project. I must
imagine the rubble they carry away and the rubble yard they
take it to.

In the rubble yard

another face is being formed, one with sponges and pimples,
one with gaskets and a fedora and a mustache, one that
can stomach the sky's drills and nails, one that needs no
medication. Its gravel eyes pierce the sun-cloud and as I lean
over to kiss it

I am transported.

My sandals are still in the closet. I hate the closet. I hate
opening it. I hate closing it. I hate putting coats in it. I hate
taking coats from it. I never leave the house.

6

"Spiral, believe me,"

I say to myself, "spiral, come out of the laboratory, out of the knotty tree stub, hold yourself before my eyes, spiral, spin me into the eggshell of oblivion, that bed sinks into the bones.

I look for you

in open books, in folded sheets, in closed cupboards, in canceled checks, in locked accounts, in roaring flames, in murmuring streams, in floating foam, in floating water, in rusty canisters and half-opened eyes.

To find you

I do nothing. I do not clean the kitchen. I do not empty the cup. My lips remain parched, the face is never built, it recoils from itself. When the stream freezes I walk across. Nothing resides there."

7

In the new spiral

the water bottle dumps continuously over my head but the
water feels like air blowing warm dust over a gas station where
the attendant has turned into a water bottle in which I see my
face.

And I see small specks

of sand and call them the stars. I wrap my hair around my fist
and punch at the invisible malady. My pocket is full of petals
freshly torn from a lilac.

Freshly torn

from a lilac. Freshly torn. A lilac freshly torn. Torn from a
town beside a lake. A torn flower from a town by a lake. Fresh
lake. Fresh town. From a lilac freshly torn. A petal torn.

INFINITE INTERIOR

The pasture you are filled with

Fills with water, exactly what

You've been waiting for,

Another mirror to put you

In your place. And as you become

What you are waiting for

What you are waiting for

Becomes what you always were.

His handshake is a dragonfly

Personality sprouts like weeds along the shore

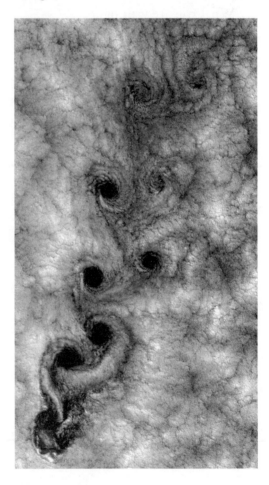

I am not a multitude and cannot splinter to follow them

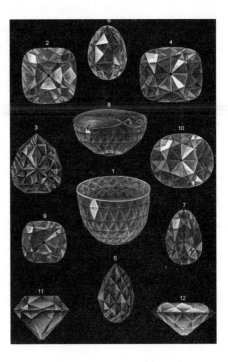

I am transported

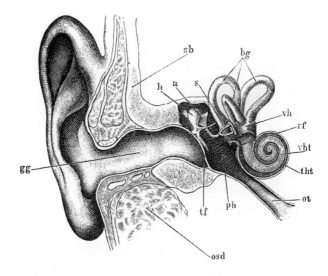

LILY OF THE INTERIOR

A lily is sprouting from my head.
First I love it, then I want it dead.

FAMILY OF THE INTERIOR

When my wife comes home from work
The invisible bird is still hissing near
Her head. She looks for the mail and wrinkles
Her nose at a waft of cottage cheese.

I'm hungry too. I open the fridge
And the bird disappears. My son
Plays alone with a tiny tuba beneath
The unopened window, the one I call

Luminous plateau, the one he calls
Atrium, that eruption of peaceful mental
Functions which halts the heretofore
Continuous progress of the tuba's tune.

I sense a nascent ache in my lower back.
My mood becomes a kind of verb.
I reach for my son, I kiss his cheek.
My wife turns off the sink.

FILM OF THE INTERIOR

Last night I watched my favorite movie
Because I wanted to forget how terrible
Love is, a gift, a crumbling leaf
Coughed up. A piece of plaster
Fell from the ceiling so I placed it
In a jar and labeled it "You" because I was
Looking for my friend on the ceiling
And I was looking for my friend in the night
And I was looking for my friend in my brain
And in the library and in the office
And in the bathroom, all of which
Held growing blotches of night.
In the morning my face rose like mist
Off a lake. Now it is snickering all the time
Because it loves you, it has this secret
Of ripped purple paper to show you,
It thinks of you as this green entity
Not entirely organic, but prelinguistic
And miles of fire stretching our visual field.

INSTITUTION OF THE INTERIOR

An anonymous institution
Was controlling my limbs
And my insides were turning
To crumbs. They reminded me
Of an old scone you can't
Even hold between your fingers
But if you could get it
To your mouth it would be
Delicious, you'd fill up
Your stomach and take a nap
In the noon light shining
Through the window,
Your greasy long hair
A pool of dark light deep
In the middle of your being.

And when the delivery truck
Comes by the building,
You wake up. You become
Another institution,
One with a name that we
Could ride a bus to, and
In fact we rode a bus to you,
We asked about your policies,
You filed a missing persons
Report because I kept
Telling you how much I wept
Without you on my side.

Now that you have
Installed a tracking device
Somewhere in the ocean

Of my skin you can find me
Whenever I am gurgling coffee
Or riding my bicycle
Along the lakefront.
And I can hear the thud
Of your footsteps and I know
Now how you know.

GOD OF THE INTERIOR

My god is the god of snowdrifts.
My god is the god of dumb beasts and rocks.
I beat on the counter,
I blast a mirror in the sandstorm,
I'm looking for my god but
My god is a quickie,
My god is a Popsicle melting on the pavement
And I'm happy I have shoes.
My god is the author of seven books of poems.
My god treads upon the ground
But laughs like a ballerina.
My god yowls in a pillow
And I yowl in a pillow and together
We are the choir of angels.
My god has bad manners, shitty syntax,
And a rusty shovel heavier than snow.
Let's help him out.
Let's buy him a snowblower.
Let's bring him a care package.
My god is the emperor of ice cream
And the prince of hate and the queen of voltage
And the whore of capitalism.
My god is a circuit breaker.
My god was born in the mouth of a slaughtered cow
And dropped in the sink by an indifferent nurse.
My god's heart is an affliction.
My god's face is an abrasion.
My god says nobody is perfect,
Nobody is holy.
Nobody can look at my god without

Feeling a wheel grinding at the ribcage.
My god is falling through the storm cloud
And needs a better parachute.
My god crawls on his belly because
My god is a saint.
My god is a suicide because
My god is a saint.
I walk around town looking
For my god in the windows
And in the bare branches
And in the bookstores
And in the dog shit.
My god lives on a fire escape.
My god has no tangible benefits to the soul.
My god is the word "No" stuck in the mouth.
My god my god every word is my god.
My god is a cutthroat.
My god consists of nothing but muscle.
My god wears too much makeup
Which blocks his pores so the sweat can't escape.
It's hard to know if I only have one god.
My god lives in the capital of pain.
My god is bored with the intellect and drunk by noon.
My god hates vegetables but eats them in emergencies.
My god is the shadow on the river.
My god is a good mother.
My god doesn't give a shit.

FAREWELL, INTERIOR

1

The interior holds out its leathery hands.
It wants to take me to California
Where technicians will construct my head,
And where the streetlights are broken yolks
And small furry things crawl up my legs.

2

I decline the offer so the interior flips a switch
Which makes my teeth cold as though
I am eating ice cubes in luminous fog.
I eat the ice cubes and the city evaporates.
Rain clouds swab my eyebrows with sleep.

3

A bee lands between me and the interior
Where a thicket has sprouted up.
When I step inside I lose the ability to think
But my ability to blow suddenly into a thousand pieces
Separates me from the interior which

4

Trembles like a newborn lamb.
Poor interior, it is only a pink thing
Puking out breast milk. It is only this
Persuasive reflex churning in
The darkening hole of myself.

5

O Interior! My wounds are your wounds!
I drizzle them over your outstretched canvas
And drill holes so the light will reach us on
The other side where a canola field
Is waiting to wrap us in its breath.

6

Dear Interior, I have no interior!
I am a shaved head turning into a field of breath,
This is the final birth and when the wind
Starts spinning a circle of leaves
An invisible man leaps out of the center.

HÔTEL L'INTÉRIEUR

When I suck on the mint I have
The sensation that there is a hotel
In my chest and it is my duty

To clean the linens and vacuum
The hallways which are lined
With Louis Quatorze mirrors.

The guests wear red tights
And smoke tobacco from the colonies.
When they fall asleep they evaporate

So I am left with these flame-shaped curtains.
I draw a bath and snuff the candle.
I am so bored with feeling.

Oblivion

The middle of your being

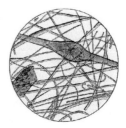

I'm hungry too

I am so bored with feeling

THE
EXTERIOR

SANDWICH OF THE EXTERIOR

Chapter 1

I woke up to the news I'd be given a free sandwich. I had
to wade through the flats and find the knob for the faucet.
It sounded horrible, like a leaf blower and a weed whacker
waltzing in a stone quarry. But for a free sandwich I was
willing to take a risk.

Chapter 2

First I took a bath and imagined a waterfall filling the
bathroom. But then I became stuck thinking about the water's
origin at the top of a mountain, how it had started as a trickle
and plummeted to this furious crashing wall. So I closed my
eyes and listened to no-tone. Whimpering grasshoppers, the
train-song, pile-driving into the anthill of my brain.

Chapter 3

That was an easy solution and I was proud of myself for
thinking of it so quickly. Now that I had my shoes on I was
hoping to find my sandwich by the docks on the other side of
the islet. Some giant milk-squirting nozzle was there, and a
man who was eating a hamburger and holding a stick. I asked
him, "Is this where the sandwiches are?" He looked at me and
chewed.

Chapter 4

I looked inside the red door and saw a frothy ocean in miniature on the third shelf. Above it were the self-help books, below it barrels of sand. I pulled a hammer off my belt and made like I was pounding nails into an invisible frame. Something started to collapse and the bus arrived.

Chapter 5

It's not clear what any of it amounted to. I stuffed the papers in the drawer and turned the lights off and on. This is maybe what was meant by sandwich. Some of the paint dried on my skin. A dog barking. Heat rising off the asphalt. I smelled anchovies.

FAMILY OF THE EXTERIOR

I thought I was climbing then the climbing became building
and I had a brick house and a family on top of a hill in a
province known for olives and glovers. That winter we burned
porcupine hides and warded off wolves with pink synthetic
feathers. Curious, intelligent, the wolves began to trust me.
Their dark eyes posed questions, and each answer opened new
questions. Sphinxlike they'd poise themselves at the windows,
watching for the feathers, licking their varnished teeth.
Eventually the sun would cross the hill and blind them with
its glare. They'd howl, so loud, so melodic, I called them my
nightingales.

WINTER OF THE EXTERIOR

Once I had nothing but a fawn that came nightly to my window, bowed her head and nibbled at the pistachio nuts I'd scatter on the ground. We had a silent understanding: every moment spent gazing in each other's eyes was a long voyage at sea. When winter came my knees began to ache. I dreamt I was water freezing and melting back and forth. There were no nights. Hopeless laughter sounded from the forest, a gray-bearded man came to drink from me. His eyes were the fawn's and when I finally awoke, birds were flying back and forth outside the window. The falling snow gave off a heavy blue light. I could not lift my legs. The sun rose. The snow rose.

MESSAGE OF THE EXTERIOR

"Your eyes are the original lacerations, and every invading photon has been a primordial sponge mopping up the fungus of your inner life. So the task is simple: pour out the box and evaporate in lamplight."

BUILDING THE SANDBOX OF THE EXTERIOR

I put on my orange shorts and dig into the ground careful
not to slice the worms in half, and as I lay down the garden
tarp I visualize a seaside resort full of tan oily bodies in
perfect rows. So I go to the beach to harvest some sand but
the beachgoers frown at the sight of a man in orange shorts
pushing a wheelbarrow. I feel as though my skin were emitting
a radioactive glow and contaminating the beachgoers and their
lunches and the granules roiling in the backwash. So I don't
dig a hole. I don't open my mouth. I pick up the shovel and
turn away.

OUTLINE OF THE EXTERIOR (THE SUN)

1. The sun rises each time I pour a glass of water.
2. Because of it, I can see all the pieces.
   a. The tools. The photos. The apple seeds.
3. Thank you, sun.
4. I'm not sure I'm anything but an eyeball.
5. And the sound of water comes from my stomach.
   a. *Inside out.* I say it to myself each morning.
      i. Drinking.
      ii. Bathing.
6. And there you are, the sun.
   a. Along for the ride, floating beside me.
   b. A friend. A theory. A performer in my picture window.
7. The sun and the dog and the shadow on the grass.
8. You have a lot of work to do.
   a. You warm up a glass of water.
   b. You evaporate a lake.
   c. And shrink a balloon.
9. How far away you are, sun, even in my chest.
   a. Where I hold you all day and all night.
   b. Where you practice swallowing my insides.
      i. Alone.
      ii. In the dark.

Their dark eyes posed questions

His eyes were the fawn's

PHOTOGRAPH © 2013 MUSUEM OF FINE ARTS, BOSTON

An original laceration

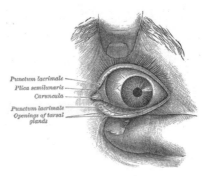

Careful not to slice the worms in half

CANDELABRA

When the baby cries it is because the light is on his head.

When the light crosses the patio, the sparrows cannot stand still.

When I drop the glass in the sink, I want to watch it shatter in the light.

The tunnel releases the eyes and pinches the light.

Alone with a tangerine: light in the backseat.

The smell of tarmac that has sat for hours in the light.

Is it possible to think darkness without also thinking light?

In the attic I was lulled to sleep by the buzzing light.

From the window to the floor, dust motes carry the light.

I used to think death was the body becoming light.

After sleeping on the beach I open my eyes to a pasture of light.

I am sitting down on top of the light; I am not killing it.

Between the CD and the coaster: the fresh patch of light.

Every night is an attempt to defy the light.

Next to the sink: wet lettuce drying in the light.

In what way is the mind a byproduct of light?

If the windows were any larger I could not stand the light.

Raindrops darting down the glass: falling prison cells of light.

THE ARCHITECT AND THE HAT

1

An architect is looking for his hat.

2

He constructs a watchtower from which he can survey the environs of his house and nearby property.

3

He designs a spiral staircase and archways that seem to disappear into the sky.

4

From the tower the architect admires the triangular trees and circular shrubs but he cannot spot his hat.

5

The hat was perhaps never real or in a blinding blue flash it vanished from his sight.

6

Though he has no idea where it is, the architect feels certain that his hat is full of wind.

7

Or of vapor.

8

The architect hates the voices he can hear from the tower's 3rd-floor window. They distract him from thinking of and looking for his hat.

9

He imagines a giant ear growing from the dirt in the courtyard.

10

The architect builds the giant ear out of fiberglass. It is not as supple as the ear he imagined and he is disappointed with its curvature, but it solves the problem of the voices.

11

Now the architect is free from voices but he misses the sound of water running and the buses he used to hear storming through the streets of the adjacent neighborhood.

12

With all this sound hullabaloo he has forgotten his quest to find the hat.

13

In a dream once more he sees the hat controlling the stream beside the pine.

14

The hat tilts to the north.

15

The goldfinches drop suddenly to the ground and the stream
freezes.

16

When he wakes up he can think of nothing but eating dessert.

17

Some ice-cream shops serve sundaes in upside-down baseball hats.

18

That's not the kind of hat he's looking for.

19

Exactly what kind of hat am I looking for? He shoves a spoonful of
cereal into his mouth and crunches slowly.

20

To assist his memory the architect constructs a room where he
assembles tiny replicas of various hats:

21

Fedoras. Berets. Derbies. Cowboy hats. Paperboy hats. Baseball hats.

22

None of them seems quite right.

23

The architect builds a narrow window to keep the outside out. He does not want the hats damaged by light or wind.

24

And he is afraid that a giant green worm will come burrow a hole in his head as though it were an apple.

25

A hat would cover up the hole.

SPORES OF THE EXTERIOR

The carpet spawns miniature cities where men and women
ride buses and subways through cavernous streets and tunnels.
And even their animals are busy, pacing in the yards, looking
at each other's eyes as if they too believed in heaven.

MARIGOLD OF THE EXTERIOR

The marigold is a feeling I get before I sleep.

A performer in my picture window

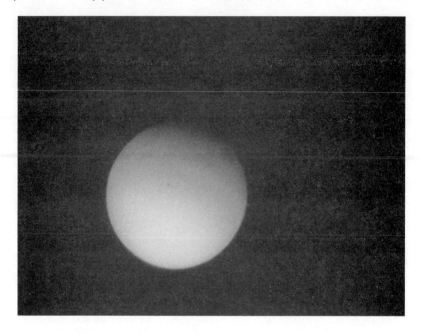

Falling prison cells of light

A hat would cover up the hole

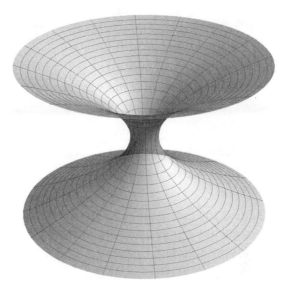

A feeling I get before I sleep

BAROMETER OF THE EXTERIOR

Sometimes I turn myself into rain.
    Airplanes still take off.
    Their motors give me shivers.

I paginate my memories.
    Falling straight to the planet
    I tear out the pictures of teats.

I curve my face around an apple.
    Silence spills from the codebook.
    The phone slips through the fingers.

The color red is a tunnel of plumage.
    I am warm there. I feel ink
    Seeping into my thigh there.

A singer steps into the automobile.
    She is full of milk and resin.
    She puts the frontal lobe on notice.

I tear out the diagram of the heart.
    A mourning dove coos at the fire hydrant.
    Droplets run in all directions.

TWITCH OF THE EXTERIOR

My left eye twitched, a communication from
The twitchy leaf detaching from the old oak tree,

Twitchy leaf about to fall to the grass, to be stomped
Into the mud or blown to another oak, to be torn

To shreds and swallowed by a rabbit, battered to
A pulp, digested and excreted, washed into

A brackish pool and smeared into the pavement—
Twitchy leaf that cannot fall asleep, cannot change

Its posture, revise its politics, sell its time, twitchy leaf
That cannot buy a book, make a note, feel despair,

Groan, belch, hesitate, burn the toast, take a bath,
Grade an essay, write a poem, rip a fingernail,

Stack the bottles in a pyramid on the patio,
Call Teddy over for fried eggs, burn the butter,

Crack the window, cut into the soft tomato
That had been sitting on the counter in the light.

SKY OF THE EXTERIOR

When sky comes out
Of the mouth
Should I break it—

Crack it open with
A spoon—spill its guts
Out on the sidewalk

Where an anthill
Was just demolished
By the three-year-old?

Militant sky ageless
And dark and swerving
Into flowers and eyes

I thought you were
Extraterrestrial but you are
An immigrant and

Something in your foot-
Step makes me stop
Frail and bloated and the

Definition of dog
Eludes me because of the
Dusk's Scotch tape

Emanation.
Refugee sky's not
An ornament or a

Brainless image flowering
In the dust cloud.
Maybe more of a clot—

Layered sky—
Dog ears up, I am your
Changeling asylum.

I am warm there

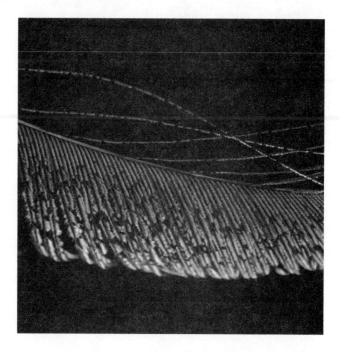

A singer steps into the automobile

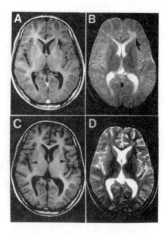

A communication

Brainless image flowering

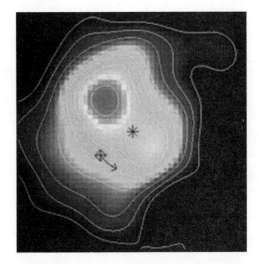

MOUTH OF THE EXTERIOR

I feel my mouth.
It is a child crying in a dark bed.

ANATOMY OF THE EXTERIOR

I feel depleted in my left ventricle
Because miniature vehicles of light
Race across the parking lot of
The convenience store where I am
Waiting for you, looking for you,
For your breath, your innumerable
Earrings spitting photons into the ether
Of my face, but I also feel so artificial,
So horribly glassy and ersatz in my
Liver and so alone in my diaphragm
That my innards are tied together
And even though the charts on my phone
Tell me which way to turn, my hands
Feel full of cold wet sand, and it's
Uncomfortable the way the stripes
On my shirt are tied together
Spitting back the light so I feel all lit up
In the optic chiasma as though
The dark marble sky were coming down
To stymie the tear ducts where
I used to believe a small family lived
And they cleared out after the first snow.

STEAM OF THE EXTERIOR

I am watching the steam come off
A team of oxen grunting
In the cold spring morning.

Soon it will snow.
Tomorrow I have to have a tooth removed
And the snow will melt

And the cold spring morning
Will be perfect for working the team of grunting oxen.
I'll watch the steam come off.

EDGE OF THE EXTERIOR

My mouth has become
The edge of me.

It spills outward
Like a spool of thread

Which I can use to stitch up
The rest of my face.

I am so afraid
Of this mouth

I keep it as far
From me as possible.

Here it is—
I hold it towards you.

ANIMAL OF THE EXTERIOR

A small animal leaps onto my chest. It spins its tail and gnashes frantically. It is free but unable to leap off me. It confuses itself with my chest hair. The ribcage imprisons it. The thuds drive its head into my guts. Its tail clutches my wrist. Its face becomes a hole spitting up the molecular void.

APPLE TREE OF THE EXTERIOR

I was in love with the apple tree, the invisible city that seemed to be growing inside it. Every time I walked by I became cloud. I liked watching myself disperse ten feet above the water tower.

*

I sat down beneath the tree to read the Poems of the Interior which I had hidden behind some fallen branches the night before. A drawing room had sprouted out of the ground. There, near the stack of paper, was an old couch and a piano and a glass of pinot noir.

*

I was building little versions of the apple tree when a breeze lifted my hat. For a moment I observed improvements in the theory of rationality. I stood in front of the orange garbage can contemplating a sandwich from the gas station.

*

On my way home I stopped at the forest to listen to all the things being born in the thickets. I have always admired that about life: it is webbed to the thicket. The branches take care of many details. Who's coming over for dinner? A sunset.

Earrings spitting photons into the ether

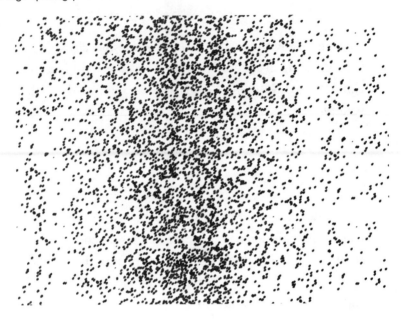

Soon it will snow

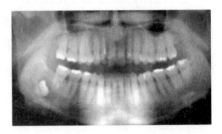

I'll watch the steam come off

Who's coming over for dinner?

HEART OF THE EXTERIOR

I should mention that my heart is a vestibule and that I cannot keep it closed. It's losing warm air and at night it looks up at me as if to say, "What is a vestibule, how come this chamber?" I will cut teeth out of the woodblocks and drop them in the vestibule. Its emptiness is my soul growing fronds, a few pines, a deciduous forest, and the dirt covers the teeth in silence.

LETTER OF THE EXTERIOR

I dread getting wet though I swim nearly every day. Water makes me feel like an exhausted word draped over a stick. When I open my mouth, a whale swims out and I am the hologram projected from its spout. From the unfading light I start comparing me to myself, which is impossible, but there's enough paper and a table and I can't help it.

I pick up the pen and write, "You are a blood-smeared lieutenant in the Royal Air Force. Now that your aircraft has crashed into a mulberry bush, it's best to wander to the seaside to collect a bag of crabs, you who will see without eyes, you who will drink without a mouth. Your teeth burn; your words are a kind of fire scorching the exterior.

"When the sun rises, it is a cannonball exploding through a window, that glassy void blocking us from the wafting river sludge and birdcalls of morning."

I tug at my socks to make certain I am still there.

I am there. The letter continues, "I send you this advice from the perimeter where mental functions take place in every organ of the body. My hair has been disloyal and I have banished it like a soul to the vegetable garden where I buried my twin brother and sister who would have turned 37 this week. Every time I swallow I become more of a wolf. The air is sobbing. The oak tree is starting to ponder my face or a star."

The letter goes on but I will never send it to the recipient, which is I, for I am an interruption and an imposture. Even my insulting cheekbone sends me into despair. I'd like to smash its atoms in a particle accelerator and drown the invisible residue in a murky puddle before locking it in a glass bottle and mounting it on the mantel so we can look up at it with a bit of terror in our veins.

"But today I am not afraid, I am looking with wonder at a man who is raising his right hand above his head. He is small and reminds me of the glass of water my son spilled at dinner last night. The glass shattered and the water soaked my salad, but I wasn't hungry and I gave the plate to the dog who ate the walnuts before falling asleep beside the mute television set. I closed the window and sat there thirsty."

MIND OF THE EXTERIOR

Where is my body?
My body is on me.

Who is my body?
My body is my self.

What is my self?
My self is the plumb line
Sinking toward the surface.

What is the surface?
The surface is a waterway.

Where did it come from?
It came from the sky.

What is the sky?
The sky is a film.

How does one watch it?
One watches it with eyes closed.

Why close the eyes?
Because the eyes are the body.

What is the body?
The body becomes light.

Where is it going?
To the other side of the couch.

When will it get there?
When morning comes around again.

Why is it a circle?
I am a circle.

What is a circle?
A way to be erased.

IMAGE CREDITS

Thank you to the photographers and artists who have agreed to let me use their images or have placed their work in the public domain. (Images on the following pages are used under the Creative Commons license: 9, 16 top, 29, 40, 41 top, 52 top, 53, 62, 63, 68, 69 bottom, 76, and 77.)

Page 8 Puddle
Page 8 Mary Louis Long (née Schultz), courtesy of the author
Page 9 Woman with camera, photograph by Alfred Cheney Johnston, 1920
Page 9 Fingerprints on a glass of water made visible by total internal reflection, by Olli Niemitalo
Page 16 Water mites in a mat of floating algae, by Jim Conrad
Page 16 Renaissance revival chair, from *Le Garde-meuble, ancien et moderne*, by Désiré Guilmard, courtesy of the Smithsonian Libraries, Washington, D.C.
Page 17 Charles Dickens, ca. 1852, by Antoine François Jean Claudet, The Library Company of Philadelphia
Page 17 Lightbulb
Page 28 Nathan Hoks, by Nicole Flores
Page 28 Clouds off the Chilean Coast (von Kármán vortex street), 1999, by Bob Cahalan, NASA GSFC
Page 29 Några stora och ryktbara diamanter, from *Nordisk Familjebok*, 1907
Page 29 Ear, from *Tidens Naturlære*, by Poul La Cour. Gyldendal, 1903
Page 40 A generic white chicken egg, by Ren West
Page 40 Pele's hairs seen through a microscope at 15 magnification, *Popular Science Monthly*, volume 48, 1895–1896
Page 41 Homemade cottage cheese from milk and vinegar, by John Shadle
Page 41 Candle
Page 52 These are the European grey wolves, out and about!, by Harlequeen
Page 52 Josiah Johnson Hawes, Self-Portrait as an Old Man, Josiah Johnson Hawes, American, 1808–1901, about 1895. Photograph, albumen print mounted on board. Image/mount: 17.2 x 12.8 cm (6 3/4 x 5 1/16 in.). Museum of Fine Arts, Boston. Bequest of W. G. Russell Allen. 2004.127. Photograph © 2013 Museum of Fine Arts, Boston
Page 52 Lacrimal papilla, from *Gray's Anatomy of the Human Body,* Twentieth Edition, 1918
Page 53 Earthworms, by Ines Zgonc
Page 62 Le soleil, au télescope
Page 62 Raindrops on window, courtesy of Frank Vincentz
Page 63 A Lorentzian wormhole, courtesy of Allen McCloud
Page 63 Marigold, courtesy of Tracy Ducasse
Page 68 Peacock plumage, by Gordana Adamovic-Mladenovic
Page 68 Subacute sclerosing panencephalitis, by Daniel J. Bonthius, Nicholas Stanek, Charles Grose/CDC
Page 69 Oak leaf
Page 69 Vega's dust cloud, NASA
Page 76 Répartition théorique photons, courtesy of Padoup-padoup
Page 76 Wisdom tooth with cyst, by Pidalka44
Page 77 Aruncuta, 1947, by Tare Gheorghe
Page 77 A flock of red-winged blackbirds flying into the sunset, by Jerry Segraves

PENGUIN POETS

JOHN ASHBERY
Selected Poems
Self-Portrait in a Convex Mirror

TED BERRIGAN
The Sonnets

LAUREN BERRY
The Lifting Dress

JOE BONOMO
Installations

PHILIP BOOTH
Selves

JULIANNE BUCHSBAUM
The Apothecary's Heir

JIM CARROLL
Fear of Dreaming: The Selected
    Poems
Living at the Movies
Void of Course

ALISON HAWTHORNE DEMING
Genius Loci
Rope

CARL DENNIS
Callings
New and Selected Poems,
    1974–2004
Practical Gods
Ranking the Wishes
Unknown Friends

DIANE DI PRIMA
Loba

STUART DISCHELL
Backwards Days
Dig Safe

STEPHEN DOBYNS
Velocities: New and Selected Poems,
    1966–1992

EDWARD DORN
Way More West: New and
    Selected Poems

ROGER FANNING
The Middle Ages

ADAM FOULDS
The Broken Word

CARRIE FOUNTAIN
Burn Lake

AMY GERSTLER
Crown of Weeds: Poems
Dearest Creature
Ghost Girl
Medicine
Nerve Storm

EUGENE GLORIA
Drivers at the Short-Time Motel
Hoodlum Birds
My Favorite Warlord

DEBORA GREGER
By Herself
Desert Fathers, Uranium
    Daughters
God
Men, Women, and Ghosts
Western Art

TERRANCE HAYES
Hip Logic
Lighthead
Wind in a Box

NATHAN HOKS
The Narrow Circle

ROBERT HUNTER
Sentinel and Other Poems

MARY KARR
Viper Rum

WILLIAM KECKLER
Sanskrit of the Body

JACK KEROUAC
Book of Sketches
Book of Blues
Book of Haikus

JOANNA KLINK
Circadian
Raptus

JOANNE KYGER
As Ever: Selected Poems

ANN LAUTERBACH
Hum
If in Time: Selected Poems,
    1975–2000
On a Stair
Or to Begin Again

CORINNE LEE
PYX

PHILLIS LEVIN
May Day
Mercury

WILLIAM LOGAN
Macbeth in Venice
Madame X
Strange Flesh
The Whispering Gallery

ADRIAN MATEJKA
The Big Smoke
Mixology

MICHAEL MCCLURE
Huge Dreams: San Francisco
    and Beat Poems

DAVID MELTZER
David's Copy: The Selected
    Poems of David Meltzer

ROBERT MORGAN
Terroir

CAROL MUSKE-DUKES
An Octave Above Thunder
Red Trousseau
Twin Cities

ALICE NOTLEY
Culture of One
The Descent of Alette
Disobedience
In the Pines
Mysteries of Small Houses

LAWRENCE RAAB
The History of Forgetting
Visible Signs: New and
    Selected Poems

BARBARA RAS
The Last Skin
One Hidden Stuff

MICHAEL ROBBINS
Alien vs. Predator

PATTIANN ROGERS
Generations
Wayfare

WILLIAM STOBB
Absentia
Nervous Systems

TRYFON TOLIDES
An Almost Pure Empty Walking

ANNE WALDMAN
Gossamurmur
Kill or Cure
Manatee/Humanity
Structure of the World
    Compared to a Bubble

JAMES WELCH
Riding the Earthboy 40

PHILIP WHALEN
Overtime: Selected Poems

ROBERT WRIGLEY
Anatomy of Melancholy
    and Other Poems
Beautiful Country
Earthly Meditations: New
    and Selected Poems
Lives of the Animals
Reign of Snakes

MARK YAKICH
The Importance of Peeling
    Potatoes in Ukraine
Unrelated Individuals Forming
    a Group Waiting to Cross

JOHN YAU
Borrowed Love Poems
Paradiso Diaspora